MY FIRST LOOK AT PETS

BIRDS USE STRONG FEET TO HOLD ON TO THINGS

Birds

Valerie Bodden

CREATIVE EDUCATION

Published by Creative Education

P.O. Box 227, Mankato, Minnesota 56002

www.thecreativecompany.us

Creative Education is an imprint of The Creative Company

Design by Rita Marshall

Production by CG Book

Photographs by Dreamstime (Andesee, Jilllang, Kitch, Mrolands, Mhprice, oneworld-

images, Phakimata, Seraphic), Getty Images (Frank Greenaway, Pete Oxford, Steve Satushek)

Copyright © 2009 Creative Education

Printed in the United States of America

Library of Congress Cataloging-in-Publication Data

Bodden, Valerie. Birds / by Valerie Bodden.

p. cm. — (My first look at pets)

ISBN 978-1-58341-721-8

1. Cage birds—Juvenile literature. I. Title.

SF461.35.B63 2009   636.6'8—dc22   2007051593

First edition 9 8 7 6 5 4 3 2 1

BIRDS

Feathered Friends

Birds are amazing animals. They fly through the air. They sing pretty songs. And they make great pets!

Birds are covered with feathers. They have strong wings. Birds have **hollow** bones. Their feathers, wings, and hollow bones let birds fly.

MANY BIRDS HAVE LONG WING AND TAIL FEATHERS

Pet birds come in many different sizes. Some are small. They can fit in the palm of your hand. Others may be almost three feet (90 cm) long!

A bird's feathers can be black or brown. They can be blue or green. Some are red or yellow. Some birds' feathers are lots of different colors!

Birds lose their old
feathers and grow new
ones at least once a year.

Choosing a Bird

There are many different kinds of birds. Some birds live only in the wild. Others make good pets.

Some people like to keep small birds as pets. Small birds are usually easier to take care of than big birds. Budgerigars (*buh-juh-REE-garz*) and finches are small birds. They are friendly and make good pets for kids.

People have been

keeping birds as pets

for more than 4,000 years.

Other people like to keep big birds as pets. African grey parrots are big birds. So are Amazons and macaws (*muh-KAHZ*). Big birds can cost a lot of money. Some of them can be very loud, too.

Bird Care

Pet birds need to be kept in a cage. The cage should be big enough for the bird to fly around in. It should have **perches** for the bird to sit on.

AFRICAN GREY PARROTS ARE BIG AND SMART BIRDS

Birds need healthy food. Some birds like to eat seeds. Others eat fruit. Some birds eat **insects**. Birds need fresh water, too.

Birds need baths. Many birds like to splash in a bowl of water. Others like to be sprayed with water.

JUST LIKE WILD BIRDS, PET BIRDS NEED BATHS

Birds need regular checkups. A **veterinarian**, or vet, checks birds to make sure they are healthy. Some pet birds live seven or eight years. Others live longer. Pet parrots can live up to 100 years!

BIRD FUN

Birds love to play. Some birds like to play with toys in their cages. Ladders and little balls make good bird toys. Some birds like to look in mirrors.

Most birds like to
have their cages covered
at night so they can sleep.

PET FINCHES LIKE TO BE WITH OTHER FINCHES

Birds need some time out of their cages every day. They need a chance to fly around. Some birds like to land on their owner's finger. Other birds might like to be petted.

Many birds can be taught how to talk. Budgerigars and African grey parrots like to talk. Saying a word to a bird many times can help it learn the word. Bird owners might even be able to teach their pets to say, "I love you!"

BUDGERIGARS ARE SOMETIMES CALLED "BUDGIES"

Hands-on: Feed the Birds

One way to learn more about birds is to watch them in the wild. Build a bird feeder to make birds come to your backyard!

What You Need

A pinecone
A piece of string about 18 inches (46 cm) long
Peanut butter
Birdseed
A plastic knife

What You Do

1. Tie the piece of string around the top of the pinecone.
2. Use the plastic knife to spread peanut butter all over the pinecone.
3. Roll the pinecone in the birdseed.
4. Hang your bird feeder outside and watch the birds that come to enjoy your tasty treat!

WILD BIRDS SPEND A LOT OF TIME LOOKING FOR FOOD

Index

Words to Know

hollow—empty on the inside

insects—small animals that have six legs

perches—branches or sticks for birds to sit on

veterinarian—an animal doctor

Read More

Bozzo, Linda. *My First Bird*. Berkeley Heights, N.J.: Enslow, 2008.

Gillis, Jennifer Blizin. *Birds*. Chicago: Heinemann Library, 2004.

Loves, June. *Birds*. Philadelphia: Chelsea Clubhouse, 2003.

Explore the Web

Enchanted Learning: African Grey Parrot http://www.enchantedlearning.com/subjects/birds/printouts/Grayparrotprintout.shtml

Kids' Bird Club http://www.birdchannel.com/kids-bird-club/default.aspx

ASPCA Animaland Pet Care: Birds
http://www.aspca.org/site/PageServer?pagename=kids_pc_bird_411